The Firefly's Light

The Secret Inventors of Our Natural World

Sarah Horne

SCHOLASTIC

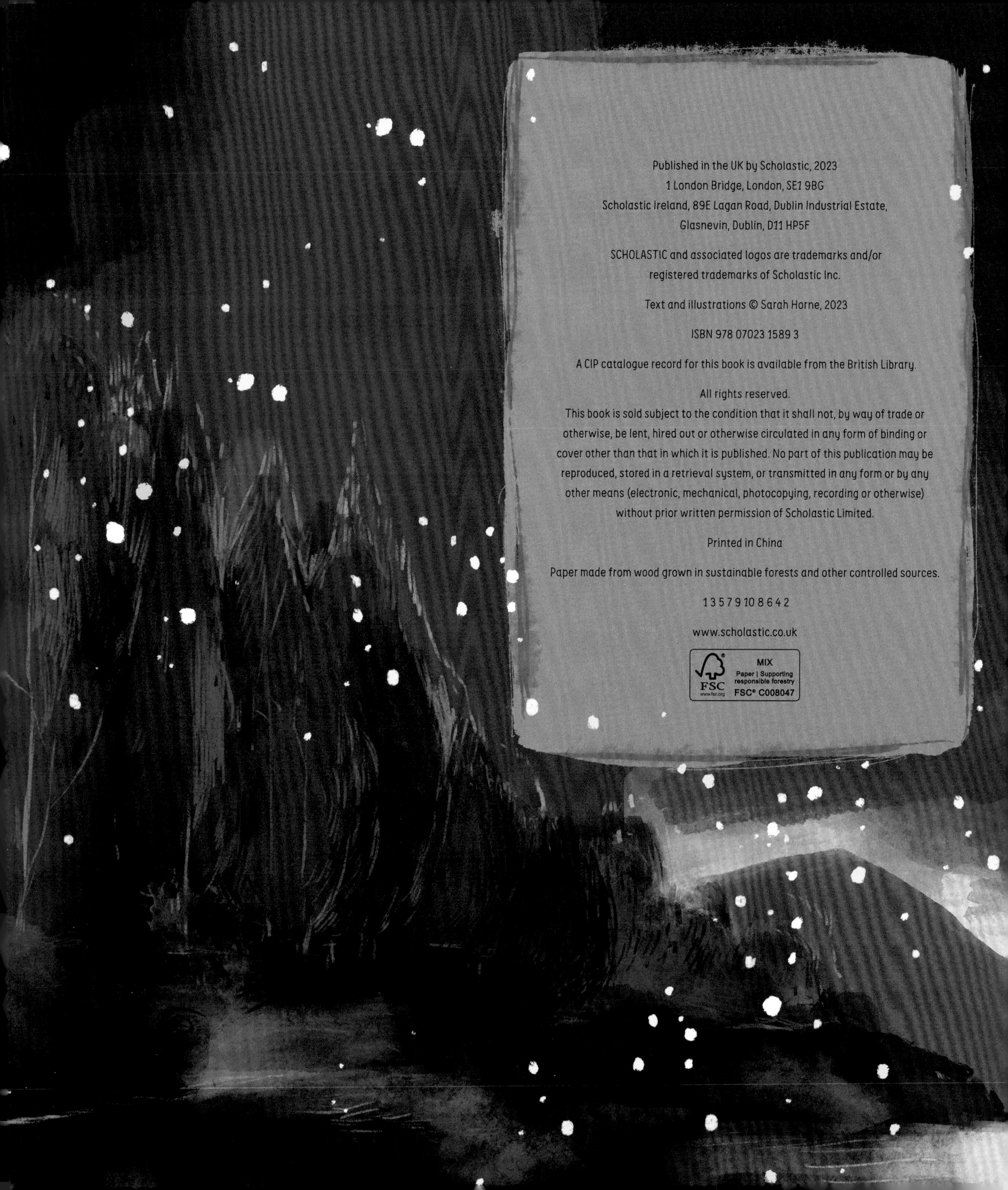

Published in the UK by Scholastic, 2023
1 London Bridge, London, SE1 9BG
Scholastic Ireland, 89E Lagan Road, Dublin Industrial Estate,
Glasnevin, Dublin, D11 HP5F

ISBN 978 07023 1589 3

A CIP catalogue record for this book is available from the British Library.

Printed in China

Paper made from wood grown in sustainable forests and other controlled sources.

1 3 5 7 9 10 8 6 4 2

www.scholastic.co.uk

CONTENTS

Introduction . . . 5

1. Bright Eyes . . . 6
2. A House with a Coat . . . 8
3. Birds and Flight . . . 10
4. Burrs and Furs . . . 12
5. The Kingfisher's Beak . . . 14
6. Another Day at the Termite Mound . . . 16
7. Leonardo da Vinci . . . 18
8. The Sailfish Supercar . . . 20
9. The Flea's Knees . . . 22
10. Hexagon Power! . . . 24
11. Antoni Gaudí and Art Nouveau . . . 26
12. Dolphins . . . 28
13. The Iron-Clad, Scaly-Foot Snail . . . 30
14. Swarm Intelligence . . . 32
15. Gecko Feet . . . 34
16. Paper Wasps . . . 36
17. The Firefly's Light . . . 38
18. Spider Silk . . . 40
19. The Elephant's Trunk . . . 43
20. Slime Mould . . . 44

And There We Have It! . . . 46

Glossary . . . 47

Index . . . 48

'It is that as existing inventions have been anticipated by Nature, so it will surely be found that in Nature lie the prototypes of inventions not yet revealed to man.

The great discoveries of the future will, therefore, be those who will look to Nature for Art, Science or Mechanics, instead of taking pride in some new invention, and they will find that it existed in Nature for countless centuries.'

REV. J. G. WOOD

'Tomorrow we will do beautiful things.'

ANTONI GAUDÍ

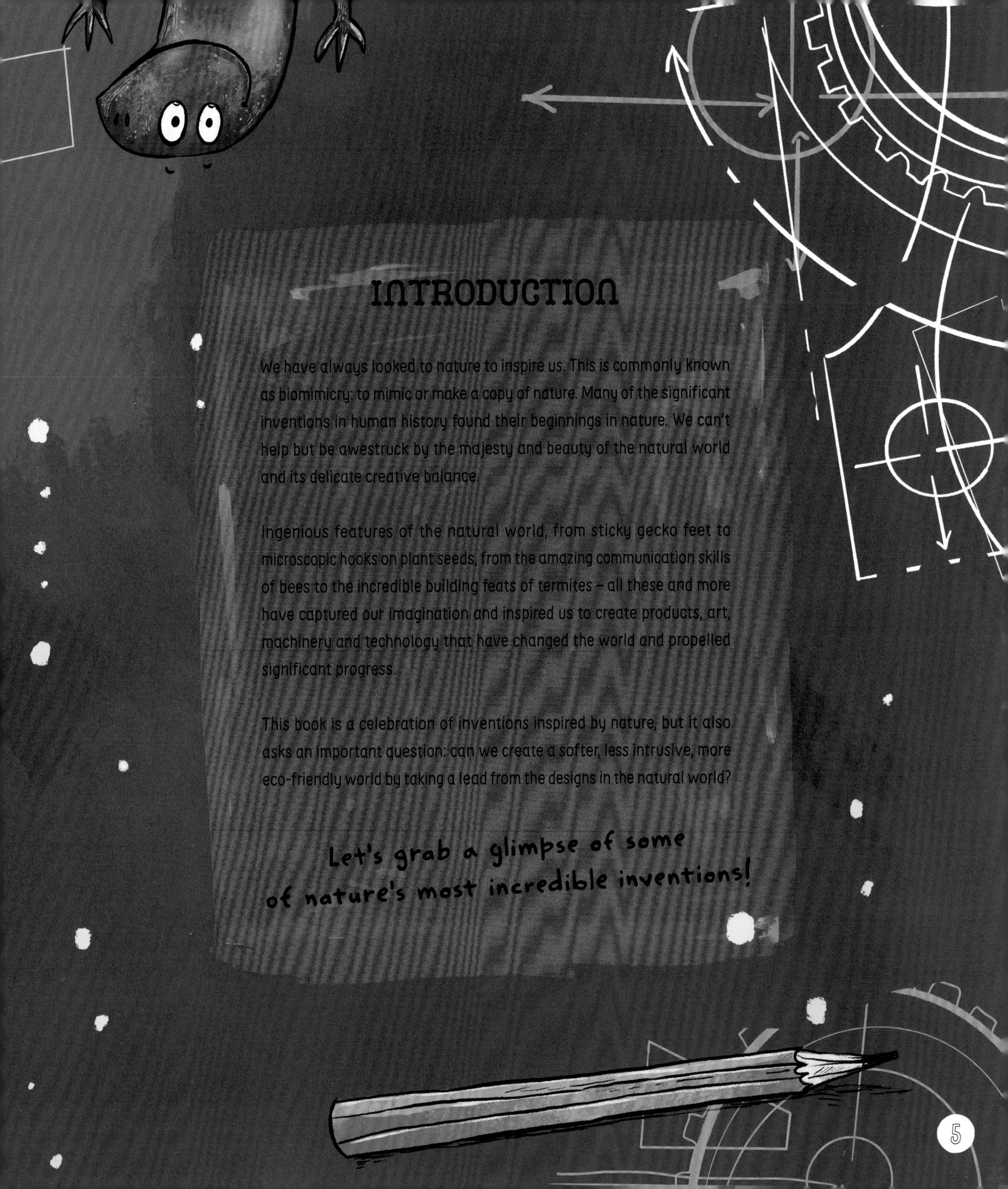

INTRODUCTION

We have always looked to nature to inspire us. This is commonly known as biomimicry: to mimic or make a copy of nature. Many of the significant inventions in human history found their beginnings in nature. We can't help but be awestruck by the majesty and beauty of the natural world and its delicate creative balance.

Ingenious features of the natural world, from sticky gecko feet to microscopic hooks on plant seeds, from the amazing communication skills of bees to the incredible building feats of termites – all these and more have captured our imagination and inspired us to create products, art, machinery and technology that have changed the world and propelled significant progress.

This book is a celebration of inventions inspired by nature, but it also asks an important question: can we create a softer, less intrusive, more eco-friendly world by taking a lead from the designs in the natural world?

Let's grab a glimpse of some of nature's most incredible inventions!

1 BRIGHT EYES

Late one night, a black cat with bright yellow eyes decided to go for a walk. At around the same time, Percy Shaw was driving his old car along the winding country roads. He was tired after a long day's work and wanted to get home. Suddenly, a thick fog engulfed his clunky vehicle, forcing Percy to reduce his speed as he strained to make out the edges of the country lane.

Just then, as if from nowhere, a pair of eyes shone out in the darkness, bright and clear, and Percy realized he was headed for a ditch! Percy swerved and avoided the ditch with centimetres to spare! The cat blinked and slunk away into the hedgerow.

A thought began to form in Percy's mind...

What makes a cat's eyes shine so brightly in the dark? An idea began to bubble up and he asked himself, 'What if...?'

Percy later discovered that the effect was called 'eyeshine', which happens in animals and humans when light is shone directly into their eyes.

In 1935, Shaw began production of his 'cat's eyes' invention. He created a small stud that sat in the centre of the road; the stud was made of glass, with a black back, and a tiny mirror inside. These studs allowed drivers to stay on course in the dark or when visibility was poor. Percy's invention was described in the UK parliament as the most brilliant road safety innovation ever produced.

Today, cat's eyes are used throughout the world on motorways and main roads. They have been modified and improved on, and now the mechanism includes a rubber wiper which cleans the lens as cars drive over them and push them below the surface of the road. The cat that went for a walk on that foggy night has helped Percy Shaw to save countless lives worldwide.

2
A HOUSE WITH A COAT
Polar bear?
More like
solar bear!

Polar bears are among the largest predators in the world. They live in a cold, harsh environment, spending most of their lives on the sea ice of the Arctic Ocean. The polar bear looks white, but actually, its skin is black, and the hairs of its thick coat are hollow and translucent. The bears look white to us because the hairs scatter and reflect light back to us. But this coat doesn't just keep the bear camouflaged on the ice, it keeps the animal warm, too. Polar bears can survive temperatures as low as -50 °C (-58 °F). Beneath their skin is a very thick layer of fat, about 10 centimetres (4 inches) deep, which acts like a layer of insulation, keeping the cold from getting to the bear's internal organs.

In 2008, German scientist Thomas Stegmaier and his team conducted a study of polar bear fur. When tracking the bears using heat-sensitive equipment called infra-red technology, they discovered that the polar bears' bodies gave out so little heat that they couldn't be detected by the infra-red sensors!

Stegmaier and his team began to study how the polar bear manages to retain so much of its body heat, even in the coldest temperatures. The team discovered that the translucent hairs allow the maximum amount of sunlight to reach the bear's skin, which is black to easily absorb the heat. The closely packed hairs trap the warm air, stopping the heat from escaping.

Stegmaier and his team joined forces with SolarEnergie Stefanakis in Germany to develop a material that could mimic the heat-saving properties of polar bear fur.

In January 2013, the *Polar Bear Pavilion* opened in the city of Denkendorf. It is completely energy self-sufficient, able to be kept warm all year round by the power of the sun alone. The roof is made up of a kind of sandwich of see-through material which is layered to provide channels for air, much like the polar bear's fur, and underneath these layers is a layer of black foil to absorb the sun, much like the polar bear's skin.

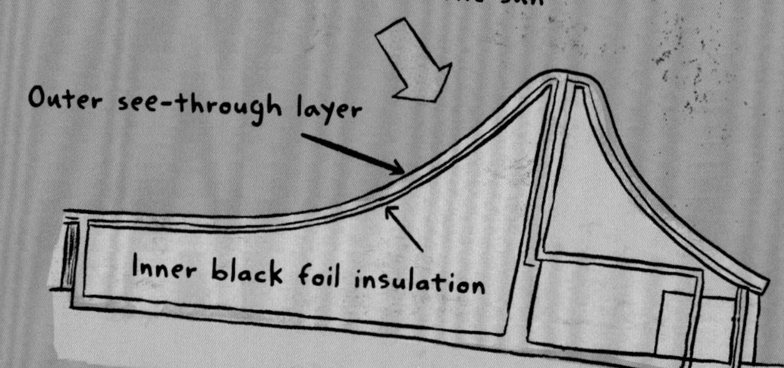

3

BIRDS AND FLIGHT

Humans have been fascinated with flight for centuries. We have watched birds soaring through the air and imagined ourselves up among the eagles, gliding between the clouds, enjoying a view like no other.

The world's largest bird is the wandering albatross, which has a wingspan of 3.5 metres (11.5 feet) and can 'wander' (fly) for incredibly long distances, often without stopping. Some records have found that the birds are capable of journeys up to 16,000 kilometres (10,000 miles) at a time. The smallest bird on the planet is the bee hummingbird, which measures just 57 millimetres (2 inches).

A bird's ability to fly depends on its flight feathers; these are attached to the wing and tail and are shaped to enable the bird to get airborne (lift) and to be propelled forward through the air (thrust) in a very controlled way.

Over thousands of years many people inspired by bird flight have tried to invent ways to allow humans to fly. They built upon one another's ideas until at last, in 1903, the Wright brothers built a powered flying machine that could actually take to the skies – and stay there!

On a windy day in the year 1010, an English monk named Eilmer of Malmesbury attached a pair of home-made wings to his arms and legs and launched himself from the top of the tower at Malmesbury Abbey. Unfortunately, he crashed straight to the ground, breaking both his legs. Eilmer walked with a limp for the rest of his life, but he had a nagging feeling he was onto something BIG.

Skip forward 800 years: a French engineer named Alphonse Pénaud created the first stable flying machine in 1871. He called it the *Planophore*. The design mimicked bird wings, but Pénaud's machine also had a tail so that it could stay balanced as it flew. On 18 August 1871 in Paris, the *Planophore* flew a distance of 40 m (131 ft), staying airborne for just 11 seconds.

The news of Pénaud's achievement spread worldwide. An American man named Milton Wright bought a model of the *Planophore* for his sons, Orville and Wilbur, who were instantly mesmerized by it. The model was made of cork, bamboo and paper, and was powered by a rubber band. Little did Mr Wright know that he had just inspired the first ever aeroplane. The world was about to become a smaller place!

The Wright brothers went on to study birds intensively, especially buzzards and the way they moved the feathers on their wingtips to stay level in the air. The brothers also drew on the work of other pioneers of flight until, finally, they designed a machine that they believed would be able to take off and fly. In 1903, they launched their 'Wright Flyer' on a beach in North Carolina, USA. They made a total of four flights, each one longer than the last. The final flight lasted 59 seconds and covered a distance of 260 m (852 ft). The modern aeroplane was born – and now an average of over 100,000 flights take off worldwide every single day.

4

BURRS AND FURS

Deep in the woods beneath towering mountain peaks, a dog ran joyfully through thicket and bramble. He loved going for walks with his master, George de Mestral, running fast and chasing interesting scents through the undergrowth – there was really nothing better!

Stopping for a break, de Mestral noticed some curious objects stuck to his dog's fur. They were seedcases from a burdock plant, called burrs. Placing a burr under the microscope, he saw that it had hundreds of tiny hooks, which allowed it to attach easily to a surface such as clothing or animal fur. The seeds would then be carried away, and eventually would fall onto the ground. De Mestral realised that this was nature's clever way of dispersing the burrs so that the plant could grow in many different places.

Inspired by this, in 1941 de Mestral invented a material called Velcro. The word came from merging two French words: *velours* (which means 'velvet') and *crochet* (which means 'hook').

Velcro is made of two different strips – one side has little hooks, and the other has tiny loops. When the two are pushed together, the loops are hitched by the hooks, and so the two sides hold together.

Velcro is used by NASA, helping astronauts get in and out of their bulky spacesuits more quickly. There is even a biological hook-and-loop system currently in development, which is designed to hold a patient's heart together during heart surgery.

Velcro remains one of the best examples of a nature-inspired invention. And it all began with a dog and that tiny seed, which planted itself in George de Mestral's imagination.

5
THE KINGFISHER'S BEAK

The clever kingfisher is not only beautifully coloured, but is also a very stealthy fisherman. Flying fast and straight, whirling his wings, it spots a fish just below the surface: a tasty treat! Its beak-first dive is clean and silent. The bird pierces the water without a single splash. Many unsuspecting fish have met their doom due to this fantastic, flying fishing machine.

Eiji Nakatsu, an engineer on the world-famous Japanese *Shinkansen* (Bullet Train), had a serious problem. Despite being the fastest train in the world, it was also one of the noisiest, and *Shinkansen* received many complaints from people living near the city track tunnels. When the Bullet Train travelled through tunnels, its high speed created a sound vortex. This pushed the air outwards at speed and caused a sonic boom every time the train emerged from the tunnel. This noise disturbed those nearby, so Nakatsu was tasked with solving this sonic-boom problem.

One morning, Nakatsu, who was a keen birdwatcher, had a moment of inspiration as he watched a kingfisher hunt for breakfast with a clean, splash-free dive. Suddenly, a strange and radical idea came to him. His trains needed a BEAK! A streamlined nose like a kingfisher's would cut through the air in the tunnels at high speed and in almost complete silence. So Nakatsu began rethinking the design of the *Shinkansen*.

The result is that the *Shinkansen* is now not only the fastest train in the world but **the quietest!** It runs at speeds of up to 320 km per hour (200 miles per hour), and people flock from all over the world to ride the famous Bullet Train.

6 ANOTHER DAY AT THE TERMITE MOUND

It is the middle of the day in East Africa; the sun beats down mercilessly on a huge termite mound, half the height of an elephant.

Like bees and ants, termites are very sociable and live in large groups. Termite colonies also have their own royal families – a king and queen that live deep underground in their own royal cell. They are very difficult to please and the queen refuses to lay eggs if the temperature isn't exactly right.

In 1991, a company called Old Mutual Zimbabwe Ltd commissioned a nine-story shopping and business centre. The problem here was that they did not want to pay for costly air-conditioning for the building – but given its location, some kind of cooling system was going to be essential. Architect Mick Pearce was appointed to build a structure that cools itself.

Looking to nature, Mick began to study those East African termite mounds.

Central air channel

Warm air rising

Outer wall

Pearce observed that the termite skyscrapers were not solid but covered in tiny holes at their base and featured a large central chimney. These mounds functioned as giant lungs, inhaling cool air and exhaling warm air throughout the day and night. Termite mounds are also made from soils which have a high thermal mass, meaning they can absorb a lot of heat without changing the internal temperature.

Drawing inspiration from these features, Pearce made his building out of large slabs of concrete and brick, which would be able to absorb a lot of the heat during the day. He placed low-power fans around openings at the base of the building to draw in cool air which would circulate around the internal spaces. As the air inside the building warms, it rises, and much like the termite mound's main chimney, the chimneys in the Eastgate Centre are there to funnel the warm air up and out through the roof, therefore keeping everything at a comfortable temperature.

Eastgate Shopping Centre in Harare, Zimbabwe, was one of the first buildings in the world to be entirely self-cooling and regulate its temperature without using expensive, energy-hungry air-conditioning. Since it opened in 1996, Mick Pearce and others have developed other buildings and offices worldwide that use designs based on the termite mound.

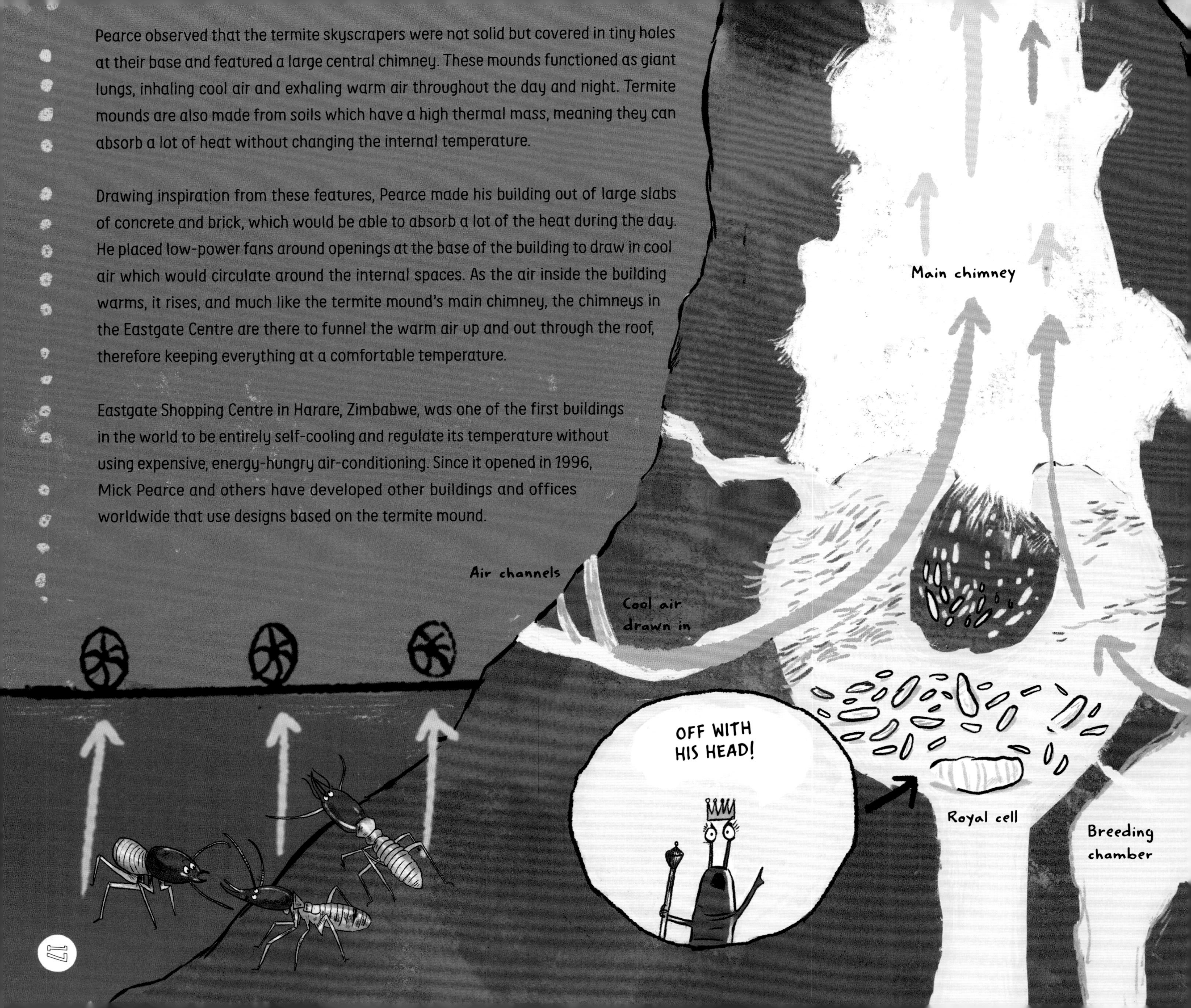

7

LEONARDO DA VINCI

TANKS AND TURTLES

Leonardo da Vinci was a man like no other. He was born in Italy in 1452 and is considered one of the greatest minds in human history. Leonardo is often described as a polymath – somebody who is very, very good at lots of different things. As well as being a brilliant artist, Leonardo was also a sculptor, an architect, a musician, a scientist and an engineer.

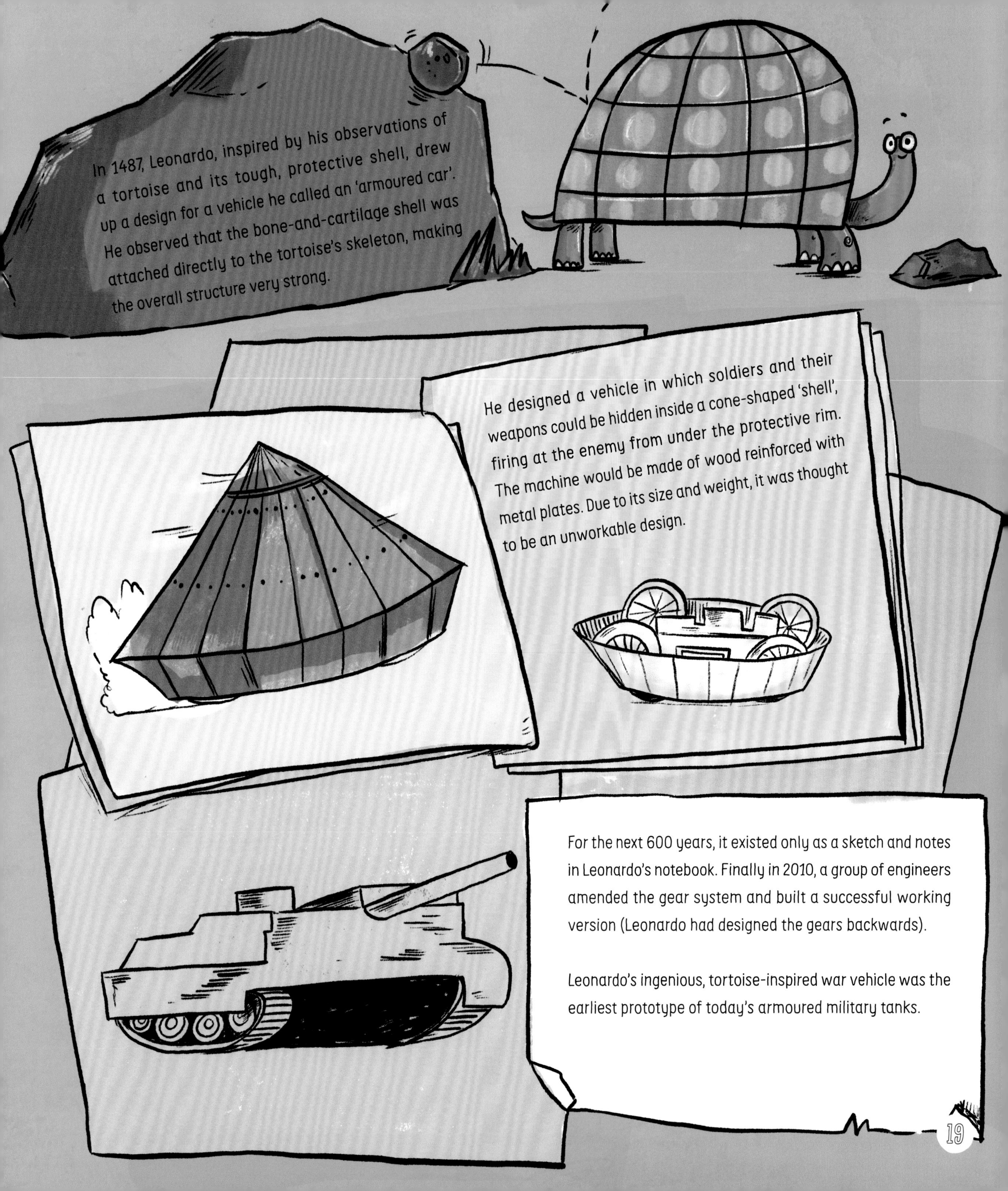
In 1487, Leonardo, inspired by his observations of a tortoise and its tough, protective shell, drew up a design for a vehicle he called an 'armoured car'. He observed that the bone-and-cartilage shell was attached directly to the tortoise's skeleton, making the overall structure very strong.
He designed a vehicle in which soldiers and their weapons could be hidden inside a cone-shaped 'shell', firing at the enemy from under the protective rim. The machine would be made of wood reinforced with metal plates. Due to its size and weight, it was thought to be an unworkable design.
For the next 600 years, it existed only as a sketch and notes in Leonardo's notebook. Finally in 2010, a group of engineers amended the gear system and built a successful working version (Leonardo had designed the gears backwards).
Leonardo's ingenious, tortoise-inspired war vehicle was the earliest prototype of today's armoured military tanks.

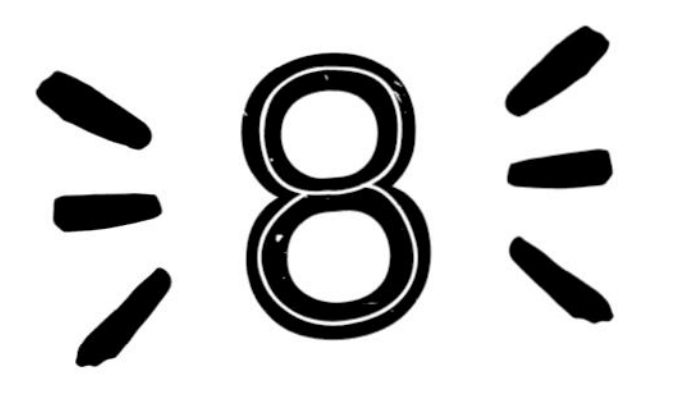

THE SAILFISH SUPERCAR

Out on the open waters of the Pacific, fishy things are happening beneath the waves. Creatures with dagger-like bills and enormous, sail-like fins on their backs are hunting schools of anchovies and sardines.

The sailfish is a kind of super-charged swordfish, capable of short bursts of incredible speed that enable it to chase down prey. They are sometimes known as the 'wolves of the sea', working in a pack to herd their dinner towards the water's surface, using it as a barrier to trap their prey.

Sailfish can grow up to 3.4 m (11.2 ft) long and are the fastest fish on Earth. They can reach speeds of up to 112 km per hour (70 miles per hour) – that's faster than a cheetah can run!

Inspiration came to Frank Stephenson, a sports car designer, while on holiday in the Caribbean. At his hotel, he spotted a stunning, multi-coloured sailfish mounted on the wall. The man who had caught the fish told Frank how proud he was to have caught it, as the sailfish was so fast. This sparked Frank's imagination, and he began to wonder what a sailfish could bring to the design table – and to the driver's seat of a supercar.

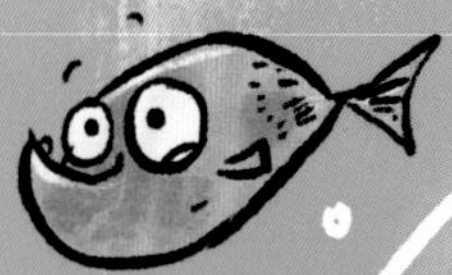

Along with the design team at racing car company McLaren, Stephenson looked in depth at the sailfish. He discovered the secrets to the fish's speed: the sailfish's scales are uniquely enabled to create thousands of small vortices (or whirls) of air as the fish moves through water. These vortices then combine so that, in effect, the fish is surrounded by one large air bubble. Water is quite dense, so when a moving object pushes the water molecules out of its way, the object loses energy. This results in drag – the slowing down of the object. With a sailfish, the air bubble produced by the vortices streamlines the fish, drastically reducing drag and enabling it to swim extremely fast. In addition to the scales, the sailfish's body has two small 'diplets', teardrop-shaped bumps, where it meets the tail fin. These help the water glide over the sailfish's body so that drag is even further reduced.

So, with the sailfish in mind, Frank Stephenson and his colleague Robert Melville designed the P1 car. The P1 has very large air ducts at the back, which are textured like the sailfish's scales. These enable air to circulate fully and freely around the engine but also significantly increases the amount of airflow to the machine. This not only helps it to run powerfully but also helps the engine cool properly, therefore increasing the car's efficiency. They also introduced diplets on the body of the car, which straighten the flow of air and further reduce drag, making the P1 one of the fastest supercars on Earth.

9 THE FLEA'S KNEES

LADIES AND GENTLEMEN, ROLL UP, ROLL UP!

The flea might be very little, but it has some SUPERHUMAN abilities, with a huge jump of 33 cm (13 in). If it were human-sized, it would be able to jump 396 m (1,299 ft), which is longer than three football pitches placed end to end. With that impressive jump, the flea would be an all-time Olympic champion. So, what's its secret?

Introducing the most wonderful, most spectacular beastie you will ever see! It's the incredible...

Torkel Weis-Fogh, a Danish scientist, discovered that the secret is in the flea's KNEES. Weis-Fogh spent many long hours in his laboratory examining fleas and other insects, including grasshoppers, cicadas and flies. In 1958, he found that all these insects had something in common: a special super-stretchy protein in their teeny-tiny knee joints called RESILIN.

RESILIN

Weis-Fogh discovered that resilin is the springiest substance around, and that it doesn't wear out or lose its shape. Resilin helps flying insects to flap their wings fast and repeatedly, and crickets to 'chirp' by vibrating the stretchy patches on their legs. And of course, resilin means that when a flea jumps, all it has to do is flex its knees and PING! It soars high into the air.

Weis-Fogh's research has got today's scientists thinking about the other possibilities for resilin.

Imagine if trainers had soles made of resilin. Anyone wearing those springy shoes could jump over a skyscraper!

Scientists are still getting to grips with this idea. Its awesomely elastic properties could be especially useful in medicine, to repair or replace damaged tissues such as vocal cords, cartilage and heart muscle. But fleas are way ahead of us! Perhaps they look at humans and wonder how high and far will we go.

IT COULD BE USED FOR...

RUBBER TYRES...

PING!

PING!

HEY!

AND SUPER BOUNCY BALLS THAT WOULD NEVER WEAR OUT...

AND EVEN... SUPER TRAINERS!

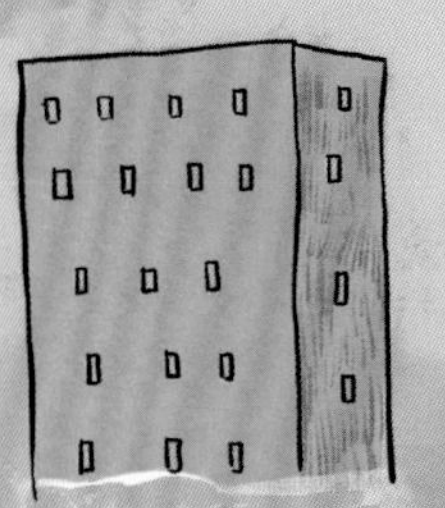

10

HEXAGON POWER!

BEES AND THE HONEYCOMB MEGASTRUCTURE

Being a bee is challenging. There is plenty of work to be done, and making honey is the name of the game. Bees feed on the sweet nectar produced by flowers and turn it into honey, which they store to eat during winter.

Inside the hive, bees make honeycombs to hold the honey, and also to protect their eggs before hatching. The walls of honeycombs are made from wax that the bees make in their bodies. It takes a long time to make the wax, so they make the honeycombs in a special shape, one that uses as little wax as possible while being super-strong – the hexagon.

Mathematician Thomas Hales is just one of the experts to have studied the science behind honeycombs made from interlocking hexagonal cells. He proved that hexagons have the biggest areas (insides) compared to their perimeters (edges). Making their honeycomb storage hexagonal means the bees can store the maximum amount of honey while making the minimum amount of beeswax for the walls. And that means more food – and more bees!

The honeycomb's structure has inspired architects and inventors throughout history. The first honeycomb-inspired structure may have been produced in China as far back as 2,000 years ago.

In 1998, Panelite, a company based in New York, pioneered the use of honeycomb structures in building materials such as ceilings, skylights, walls and roofs. Their focus was on efficiency and providing beautiful and elegant materials while conserving energy and resources.

So many other buildings around the world are inspired by the honeycomb. And as these incredible structures rise up out of the ground, the humble honeybee quietly and busily forages among flowers, makes wax and builds its home, totally unaware of its immense impact on the human world!

11

ANTONI GAUDÍ AND ART NOUVEAU

You don't have to look very far to find incredible patterns, colours and designs in the natural world; from spiral snail shells to hexagonal honeycombs made by clever bees, and from the shapes and shades of autumn leaves and summer flowers to the symmetrical patterns of ripples on still water.

Antoni Gaudí, an architect born in Spain in 1852, was fascinated by nature and drew his inspiration from it. A deeply religious man, he believed that God, in the form of nature, was the best designer. His work broke with past traditions in architecture and took building design to new heights. His masterpiece is a cathedral in Barcelona called the *Sagrada Familia* (Holy Family). Today, it is the most visited monument in Spain and is a UNESCO World Heritage Site, even though the construction of it is yet to be completed!

The building is full of reminders of the beauty Gaudí found all around him: the church's columns are inspired by spirals and tree shapes, the gates are shaped like honeycombs, friezes (decorative bands along walls) feature twisting vines, and the spires resemble tall grasses and rock crystals. Gaudí used ceramics, stained glass, wrought ironwork and intricately carved wood to recreate natural forms in his building.

Casa Batlló stands in the centre of Barcelona. It was commissioned by the Batlló family, who wanted a house that would stand out from the rest and be known for its creative design. They asked Gaudí to come up with a 'risky plan', and he certainly did that! *Casa Batlló* has very few straight lines in its structure. The outside, decorated by mosaics and broken pottery, was inspired by the human body, with skull-like balconies and supporting pillars that look like bones.

Inside, the spirals on the main floor's ceiling and pillars recreate the constant swirling and spiralling of water and wind. The focal point is a unique, mushroom-shaped fireplace. Everywhere, there are flowing lines and organic shapes. The house seems more like a living organism than a building. Gaudí took the elegance and clever designs he saw in the natural world and used them to rewrite the rules of architecture. He summed up his philosophy when he said, 'Tomorrow we will do beautiful things.'

12

DOLPHINS

In ocean waters and some rivers, playful, cheeky dolphins can be found. Dolphins are brilliant swimmers and very sociable, communicating through whistles, clicks, squeaks and squawks. They are highly intelligent and are among the few animals, along with apes and humans, to recognize themselves in the mirror!

Engineers building boats and submarines had to contend with the fact that water is far denser than air. This meant that for a vessel to be able to move through the water without the need for huge amounts of fuel, it needed to have a streamlined shape. So the engineers looked to dolphins and their streamlined, aerodynamic body shape for inspiration.

In 1804, aerodynamics pioneer George Cayley noted that a sideways teardrop shape, similar to a dolphin's body, is the perfect shape to power through dense water. Caley's findings later inspired the design of a submarine called the USS *Albacore*, which pioneered the 'teardrop hull', also known as the 'Albacore hull'. This clever design allowed for maximum speed in water and amazing manoeuvrability!

Dolphins make sounds at lots of different frequencies – from very high-pitched squeaks to low chirps. These sounds cut through the ocean's noise and dense water, helping them to seek out fish and squid, which dolphins love to eat. This communication and tracking technique is called echolocation. It is a type of built-in sonar which dolphins use by emitting sound pulses and waves that bounce off their prey. The reflection (or echo) of the sound waves reveals the prey's shape, size and location.

The dolphin sends out sounds and listens for the returning echo to find out where their next meal is.

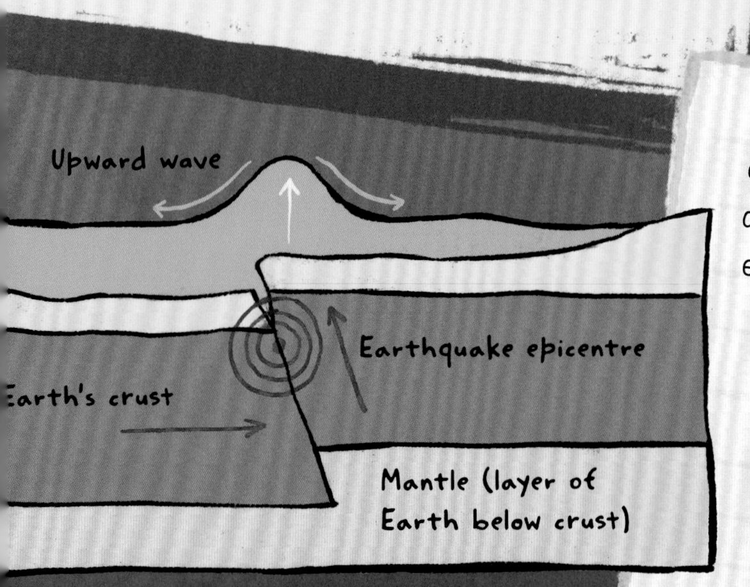

A tsunami is a huge, fast-moving ocean wave, caused by an underwater earthquake or volcanic eruption. Tsunamis can cause complete devastation to islands or coastal areas, so an early warning system is essential to allow people enough time to get clear of the danger area.

This is where the second piece of dolphin-inspired technology comes in. S2C Technology, inspired by the dolphin's chirps and clicks, designed sensors that can cut through the noise of the ocean, even on stormy days. It provides information on changes in pressure and detects underwater earthquakes that cause tsunamis, therefore helping communities on land to prepare and evacuate the space before the giant waves roll in.

13

THE IRON-CLAD, SCALY-FOOT SNAIL

Deep, deep below the Indian Ocean, an enormous ridge spans from the top of Africa down to the centre of the vast ocean. It is a harsh, dangerous place to live for a small snail, with deep-sea volcanoes sending out superhot jets of water, full of minerals. But the scaly-foot snail is not fazed as it watches out for its mortal enemy – the crab. They have been known to be locked into battle for days, as the crab nemesis latches on and squeezes the snail's shell, aiming to crush it so that it can get at the snail's soft, tasty flesh. But the snail almost always escapes being eaten because of its secret weapon in this battle – a suit of iron armour!

The snail's shell and the scales covering its foot contain iron, which the snail absorbs from the mineral-rich water around it. This means its body can withstand huge amounts of pressure from a hungry crab that's not about to give up easily! The scaly-foot snail is the only organism we know that uses iron in this way. This is one tough snail.

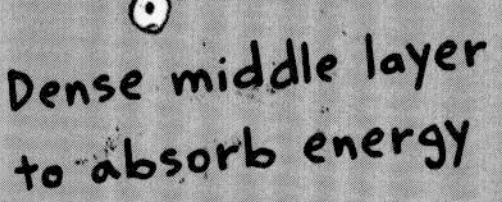

In 2010, the scaly-foot snail inspired professor and scientist Christine Ortiz and her team at MIT (Massachusetts Institute of Technology). In the lab, they replicated the squeezing motion of a crab to study how the make-up and shape of the shell allowed it to survive such intense, sustained pressure without cracking.

Christine and her team's research into the scaly-foot snail's shell helped the development and design of protective headgear for humans. Bicycle and motorcycle helmets are made to be lightweight but strong enough to withstand high impact. These deep-sea snails and their natural armour have helped to prevent many serious injuries – and even saved lives!

14

SWARM INTELLIGENCE

Many animals live or travel together in groups of hundreds or even thousands: bees, ants and termites live in colonies; birds flock together; and fish form huge swimming groups called schools. Some birds, such as starlings, display a behaviour called murmuration, which is when they all fly and swoop together, making intricate shapes and patterns in the air. But how do the individual starlings know where to go so that they don't fly into each other? How do they all change direction at the same time?

In 1989, Gerardo Beni and Jing Wang studied starlings and other animals and came up with the term 'swarm intelligence' to describe their behaviour.

Swarm intelligence means that the group members work as one for the sake of everybody. For example, in the Brazilian rainforest when the rivers flood, fire ants work together to form ladders, chains and even floating rafts from their own bodies. They become like a single super-organism, which ensures that most of the colony members survive the flood.

The study of swarms has also inspired scientists working in robotics. The Colias Microrobot was built in a laboratory in Lincoln, UK, and was inspired by a type of swarming insect called a locust. Locusts have detectors that sense movement around them. This helps them react quickly to escape danger – or avoid embarrassingly crashing into each other when they fly in a swarm! The Colias Microrobot has three short-range sensors that detect obstacles and allow the robot to move around without crashing into things.

Swarm intelligence is a hot topic for today's scientists – for instance, it's inspiring the technology behind making self-driving cars safer to use. This field is developing fast, so watch this space!

15

GECKO FEET

The most extraordinary thing about a gecko is its FEET. These seriously sticky structures are covered in thousands of tiny hairs called *setae*. Through a microscope, you can see that each hair has hundreds of triangular structures called *spatulae*. The *setae* and *spatulae*, when pressed together, produce a sticking force strong enough to hold the gecko's whole weight. These magic structures alone mean that the gecko can run up a wall or hang upside down, without the help of sticky slime or gooey glue.

Different geckos have different shaped toes to help them grip to different surfaces.

Biologist Duncan Irschick and his team at the University of Massachusetts were studying glues and adhesives and found that they all had drawbacks; many were non-reusable and eco-unfriendly; also, they couldn't be removed without leaving a sticky mark or damaging the surface.

So the team developed a completely new kind of adhesive – and their inspiration came from the gecko! They came up with an adhesive product called GeckSkin. The team replicated the gecko's *spatulae* and *setae* by weaving together a soft pad made of material such as polyurethane and a stiff fabric such as carbon fibre.

The product is spectacularly sticky: on a smooth surface, one piece about the size of two credit cards can hold up 318 kg (700 lbs). This means it's perfect for keeping large, heavy things, such as a television, stuck to a wall. It can also be removed easily without leaving marks or damaging surfaces.

Geckos mostly live in hot countries, so it's important that their feet stay sticky even when the air is humid. Just like geckos' feet, Irschick's adhesive gets even stickier in humid places, so it can also be used to seal cracks around bathtubs to prevent leaks.

The little gecko has no idea that its extraordinary sticky, hairy feet has inspired such an ingenious invention!

16 PAPER WASPS

Wasps may be annoying when you're having a picnic, but they are essential to our world. They are ecologically important predators and eat dragonflies, centipedes, beetles and moths. They are also excellent pollinators, enabling flowers and our food crops to grow. Wasps are found in every continent except Antarctica – it's far too cold for them there, plus there's a shortage of ice creams and fizzy drinks!

A wasp nest can house up 50,000 wasps (that's a lot of stings!), and paper wasps make their homes out of – you've guessed it – paper!

Otherwise known as the vespid wasp or umbrella wasp (due to the shape of its nest), this insect makes paper for their nest by chewing up wood bark and mixing it with their saliva.

Human papermaking dates back to at least 3000 BC. Ancient Egyptians removed the leaves from the papyrus plant, mashed their inner pith, then wove them together to make thin sheets. This created a very coarse, rough type of paper, but it was better than nothing!

By the early seventeenth century papermaking had moved on. In the east paper was being made from bamboo fibres, in the west they mostly used old rags, which was still very coarse and expensive. French biologist René-Antoine Réaumur began to look at paper wasps and how they made their nests. He noted that they used wood to make pulp – and that the result was a much smoother paper than human-made types.

The need for even more eco-friendly packaging has led to further developments based on wasps' papermaking techniques. Companies have begun to experiment using sawdust, a waste product from the timber industry, as an additive within 3D printing. Further work still needs to be done to eliminate the use of plastic in the binding fluid, but using waste wood powders in printing could help us to move towards a greener, more sustainable world, all thanks to the ingenious little wasp!

17

THE FIREFLY'S LIGHT

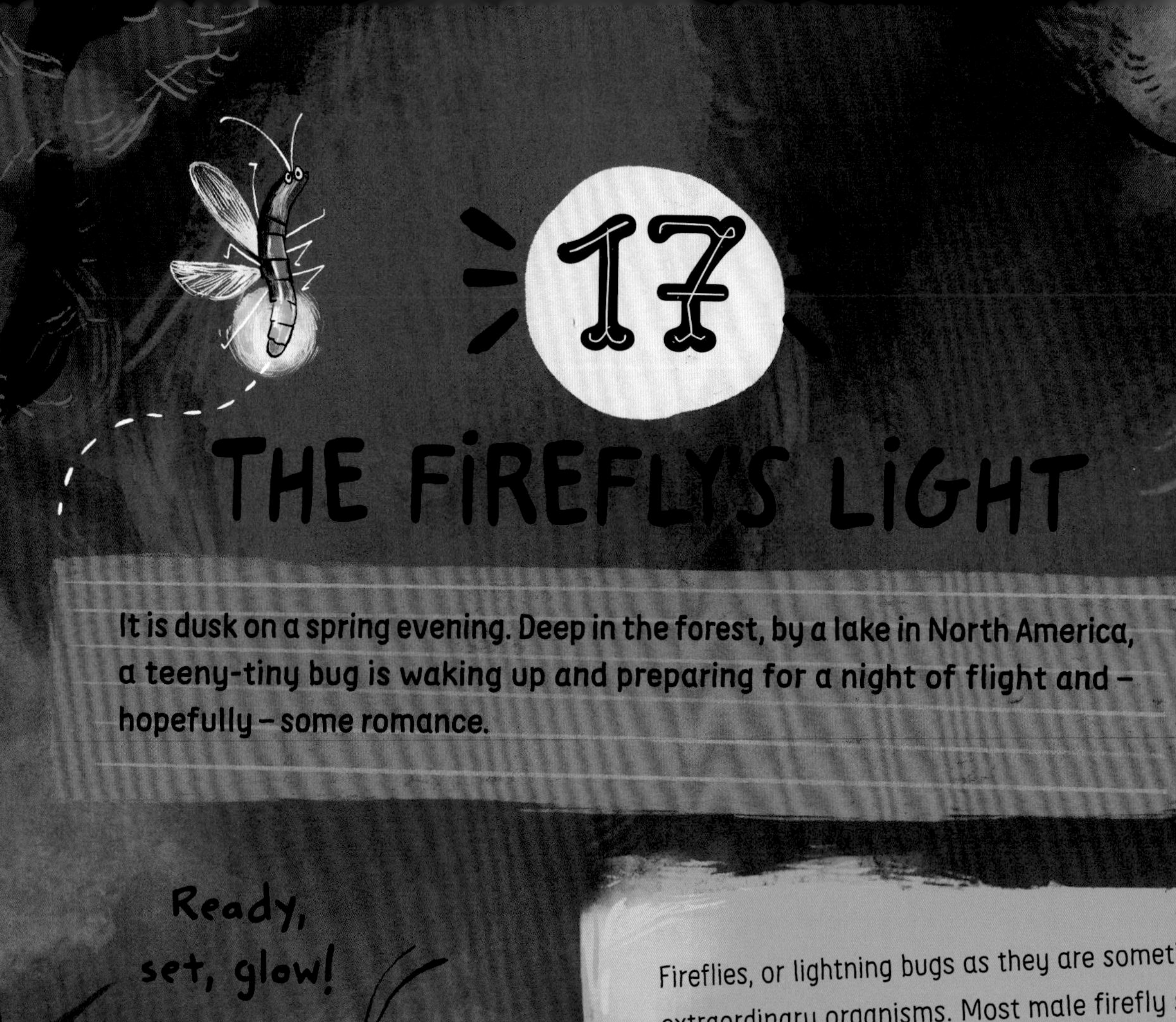

It is dusk on a spring evening. Deep in the forest, by a lake in North America, a teeny-tiny bug is waking up and preparing for a night of flight and – hopefully – some romance.

Fireflies, or lightning bugs as they are sometimes called, are extraordinary organisms. Most male firefly species glow to attract a mate, and, in some species, the female will also glow in response to the male's signal. Fireflies produce this cold light (which means light that has no heat) through a process called bioluminescence, which also occurs in some deep-sea fish, jellyfish and plankton. Bioluminescence happens when a chemical called luciferin mixes with oxygen inside the firefly's body. A jagged layer of scales on its abdomen then spreads out (refracts) the light, making it glow brightly.

LEDs are the kind of lights you might find on your Christmas tree or at a birthday party. Though much safer than the lighting of the past, the problem with these lights is that they use too much electricity and become very hot. So, a team of engineers and biologists are looking for ways to make these bulbs better.

LEDs create light by passing an electrical current through them, with different chemicals that coat the bulb making different-coloured glows. LEDs can be up to 90 per cent more efficient than traditional light bulbs, but scientists are looking for ways to make them even more efficient. Researchers are looking to fireflies for this solution. By copying the light-scattering surface of the firefly's abdomen, they have found that this increases the light's energy efficiency by 50 per cent. Research continues, but with the urgent need for us to conserve the Earth's resources, the new firefly-based light bulb may be coming to a room near you soon!

18

Spider Silk

The spider is a common sight in most countries, and there are around 50,000 spider species worldwide. Did you know that although many spiders don't spin webs, they can all make silk?

Some spiders make circular silk nests that even have doors; these nests are waterproof and shelter the spiders and their eggs from the elements. They also make perfect hiding places in which to wait for prey to pounce on. Silk can provide protection from flooding and can help to regulate the temperature and humidity of the burrows.

Sheet web

Orb web

Funnel web

Spider silk has some remarkable properties. It has been proven to be five times stronger than steel when compared by weight, and three times stronger than synthetic fibres that are currently used in aerospace and military fabrics. It's finer than human hair while being more resilient than any synthetic material, not to mention biodegradable.

Humans were also using it medicinally for centuries. It was believed that silk had anti-microbial properties, and the ancient Greeks used it as a sort of plaster on wounds, to stop bleeding and keep them clean.

In 2019, researchers and innovators in China designed a strong and stretchy material using hydrogel fibres, which are made up of mostly water, that mimics spider silk. This artificial silk has the potential to be used to make super-strong ropes and nets, helicopter ladders and parachute cords, due to its incredible shock-absorbing properties.

Some scientists in Connecticut have even started looking into using spider silk as a replacement for metal plates and screws in surgeries to repair broken bones due to its strength and elasticity. The possibilities are endless!

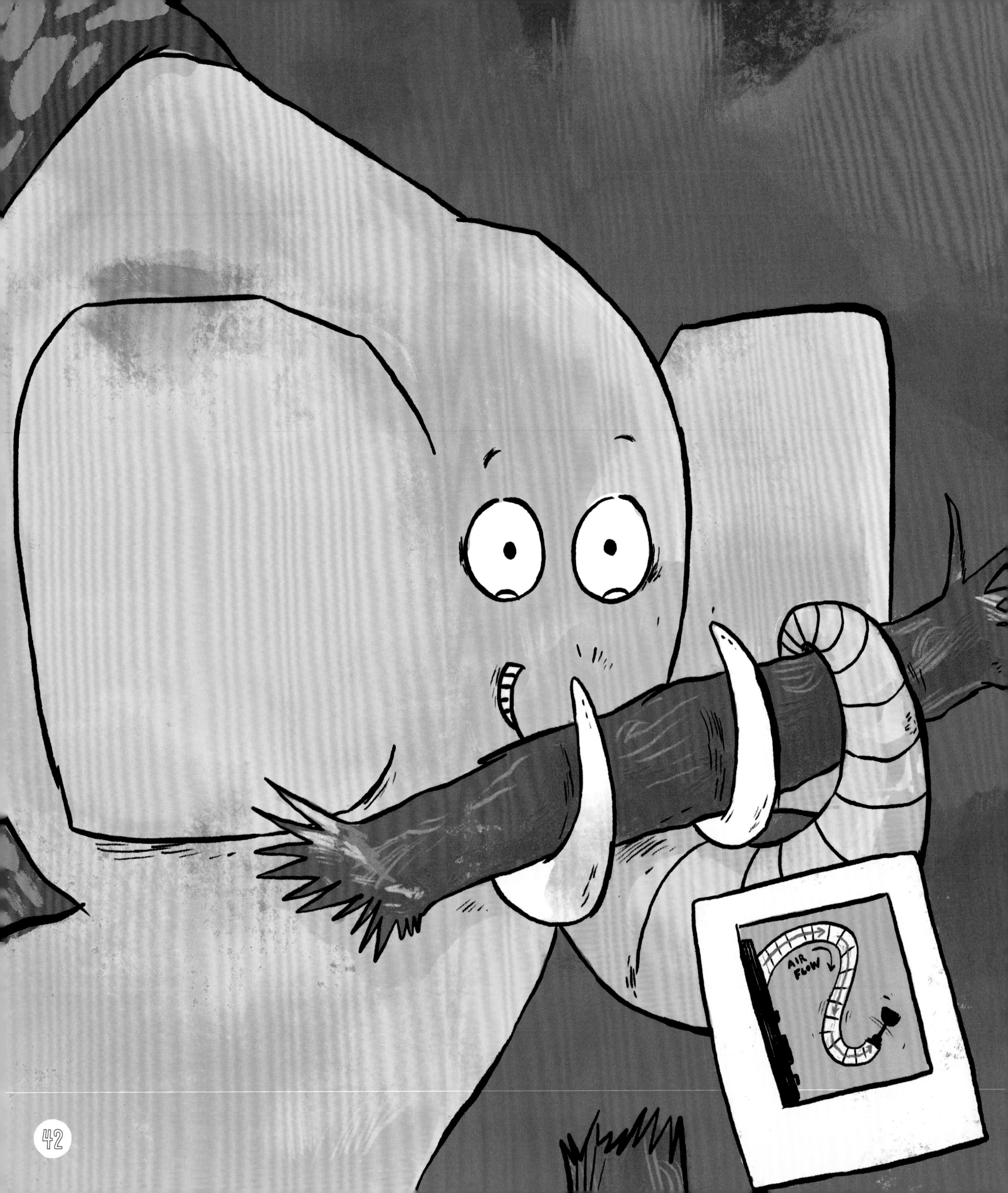
AIR FLOW

19

THE ELEPHANT'S TRUNK

SOFT ROBOTICS

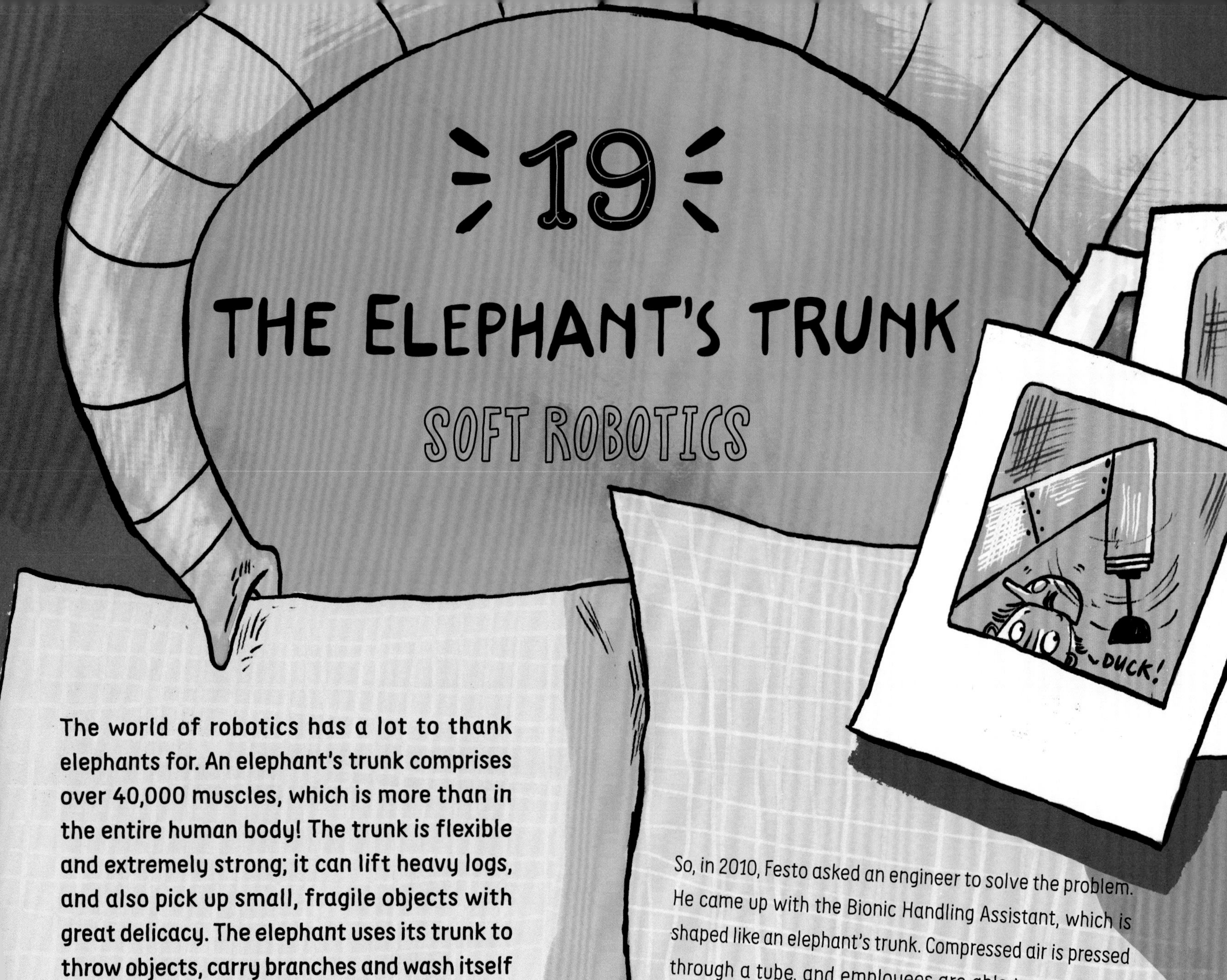

The world of robotics has a lot to thank elephants for. An elephant's trunk comprises over 40,000 muscles, which is more than in the entire human body! The trunk is flexible and extremely strong; it can lift heavy logs, and also pick up small, fragile objects with great delicacy. The elephant uses its trunk to throw objects, carry branches and wash itself by squirting water like a hose. Elephants even use their trunks like snorkels when they swim or wade in deep water.

German manufacturing company Festo had a problem with the mechanical arms on their assembly lines. They were very large, heavy and extremely rigid. This meant that workers struggled to accurately manoeuvre the arms to perform delicate tasks and were often hurt if they were struck accidentally by them.

So, in 2010, Festo asked an engineer to solve the problem. He came up with the Bionic Handling Assistant, which is shaped like an elephant's trunk. Compressed air is pressed through a tube, and employees are able to control the flow of air in order to make it shift and change direction, making it as flexible as an elephant's trunk. It also has a hand and a gripper, which Festo nicknamed the 'third-hand system', to perform delicate tasks, pick up heavy objects and manoeuvre difficult spaces just like an elephant's trunk.

The arm is made from polyamide, which is often used for making carpets and sportswear. Because of its soft feel, if workers get hit by the machines it is unlikely to cause a serious injury.

20 SLIME MOULD

BRAINLESS COMPUTING

Slime moulds are a large single-celled organism that look like gelatinous 'slime'. There are more than 1,000 different species of slime mould, and they can be found all over the world – wherever they can feed on the bacteria, yeasts and fungi that grow on dead plants. Slime mould is always in search of more food. Despite having no brain, slime mould is able to expand and ooze its way through undergrowth and debris to find a food source.

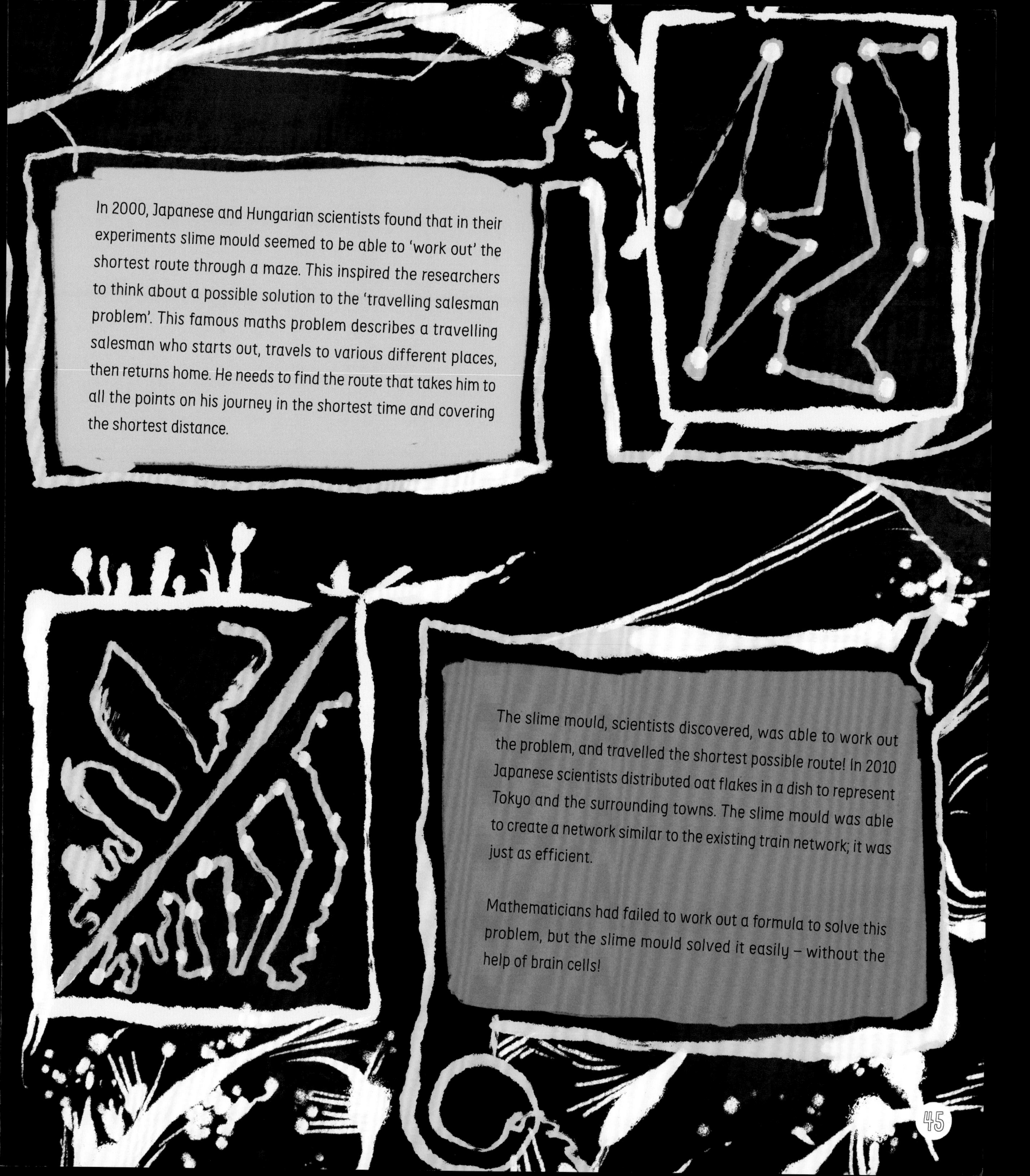

In 2000, Japanese and Hungarian scientists found that in their experiments slime mould seemed to be able to 'work out' the shortest route through a maze. This inspired the researchers to think about a possible solution to the 'travelling salesman problem'. This famous maths problem describes a travelling salesman who starts out, travels to various different places, then returns home. He needs to find the route that takes him to all the points on his journey in the shortest time and covering the shortest distance.

The slime mould, scientists discovered, was able to work out the problem, and travelled the shortest possible route! In 2010 Japanese scientists distributed oat flakes in a dish to represent Tokyo and the surrounding towns. The slime mould was able to create a network similar to the existing train network; it was just as efficient.

Mathematicians had failed to work out a formula to solve this problem, but the slime mould solved it easily – without the help of brain cells!

AND THERE WE HAVE IT!

What an amazing glimpse into nature's secret inventors.

So, let's look after our natural world, let's enjoy it and get inspired by it. Let's go outside and look closer. What if we can look to nature to solve some of the world's biggest problems? And, drawing on this inspiration, what if we can find more planet-friendly ways of doing things? After all, the natural world has been inventing long before we came on the scene!

Watch the birds, enjoy the beach, walk your dog and see what he has in his fur ... and who knows? The answers to some perplexing problems could be hiding at the bottom of the ocean, on the rainforest floor or within an elephant's trunk!

Just look out for that cat in the road...

GLOSSARY

Aerodynamic Having a shape which reduces the drag from air moving past, meaning an object can move faster.

Biodegradable A substance or object that can decompose naturally, when bacteria feed on it.

Bioluminescence The emission of light from living organisms, caused by a chemical reaction inside their bodies.

Biomimicry The design and production of materials, structures and systems that mimic those found in the natural world.

Cartilage A flexible tissue found in animals and the human body.

Compression Making a thing smaller and more compact by applying pressure.

Dispersing The action of sending out things or people over a wide area.

Drag A force acting in the opposite direction to the motion of an object moving in water, air or any fluid.

Efficiency The quality of doing something well with as little waste of energy, time or money as possible.

Eyeshine The reflection of light on the inner surface of an eye through the pupil so that the eye has a luminous appearance (as in a cat).

Frugal Sparing or limited.

Fusion Joining or blending two or more elements to form a single object.

Gelatinous A substance that is like jelly.

Generations The average length of time between parents and the birth of their children.

Hexagon A shape that has six straight sides.

Innovation A new method, idea or product.

LED Stands for 'light-emitting diode'. A diode in an electrical circuit is a part that allows an electrical current to travel in one direction.

Manoeuvrability Able to be moved easily while in motion.

Mathematician An expert in or student of mathematics.

Mesmerize Capture the complete attention of (someone).

Microscope An instrument used for viewing very small objects, it typically magnifies several hundred times.

Mimic An action or animal, plant or human that copies another.

Murmuration Usually a large group of birds that fly together and change direction in intricately coordinated patterns in the sky.

Organism An individual animal, plant or single-celled life form.

Papyrus *1.* A tall plant, a type of grass that grows in or near water, especially in North Africa. *2.* The name for paper made from this plant.

Predators An animal that lives mostly by preying on and eating other animals.

Prosthetics *1.* An artificial feature or piece of flexible material applied to a person. *2.* The branch of surgery concerned with the making and fitting of artificial body parts.

Prototype The first version of an invention.

Resilin Elastic material found in insects, especially in hinges such as legs or wings.

Sonar A system for the detection of objects underwater by emitting sound pulses and detecting or measuring their return after being reflected.

Streamlined Having a shape that presents very little resistance to the flow of air or water.

Torso The trunk of the human body.

Tsunami A long, high sea wave caused by an earthquake or other underwater disturbance.

Volatile Liable to change rapidly and unpredictably, especially for the worse.

Vortex A whirling mass of fluid or air, such as a whirlpool or whirlwind.

INDEX

A

adhesives 34–35

aerodynamics 15, 21, 28–29

aeroplanes 11

architecture 9, 16–17, 25, 26–27

B

bee hummingbird 10

bees 24–25

bioluminescence 38

biomimicry 5

Bionic Handling Assistant 43

birds 10–11, 14, 15, 32

burrs 12

C

cars 21, 33

Casa Batlló house 27

cat's eyes 6–7

computing 45

D

dolphins 28–29

E

echolocation 29

elephants 42–43

eyeshine 7

F

fire ants 32

fireflies 38–39

fleas 22–23

flight 10–11

G

Gaudí, Antoni 26–27

geckos 34–35

H

headgear, protective 31

heat conservation 9

honeycomb structure 24–25, 27

hydrogel 41

I

insulation 9

iron 31

K

kingfishers 14, 15

L

LED lights 39

Leonardo da Vinci 18–19

locusts 33

M

McClaren P1 super-car 21

medicine and surgery 13, 23, 41

murmurations 32

P

papermaking 36–37

papyrus 37

polar bears 8–9

polyamide 43

polymath 18

prosthetics

R

resilin 23

road safety 6–7

robotics 33, 43

S

S2C technology 29

Sagrada Familia cathedral 26–27

sailfish 20–21

seed dispersal 12

self-cooling buildings 16–17

self-driving cars 33

shells 19, 30–31

Shinkansen (Bullet Train) 14, 15

silk 40–41

slime mould 44–45

snails 30–31

solar energy 9

sonic boom 14

spiders 40–41

starlings 32

submarines 29

super-stretchy substance 23

swarm intelligence 32–33

T

tanks, armoured 19

termite mounds 16–17

tortoises 19

tsunamis 29

V

Velcro 12–13

W

wandering albatross 10

wasps 36–37

Wright, Orville and Wilbur 10, 11